MW00587952

Barefoot Crossing

Barefoot Crossing by Deb Grant

Copyright © 2022 by Jazzwater. All rights reserved.

Scripture quotations are from New Revised Standard Version Bible: copyright © 1989, 1995 National Council of the Churches of Christ in the United States of America. Used by permission. All rights reserved worldwide.

ISBN: 978-1-7372181-0-4

Jazzwater

Houston, Texas

Barefoot Crossing

100 + 1 Conversations with God

debgrant

Jazzwater
Houston

To Cindy

Table of Contents

Foreword

By Pastor Cindy Beck

Like every Lutheran prepubescent with determined parents, I was carted off to Confirmation on Saturday mornings. We sat on cold metal folding chairs in a poorly lit room with a pastor just as unhappy to be there as we were. The emphasis placed on Luther's catechism was "FEAR and love God." The bible said God was Almighty, Most High, Omnipotent & Omnipresent, Powerful, Avenging, Jealous, and Judge. Correct prayer required finger-entwined hands, head bowed, and focused.

That kind of prayer and relationship did not work for me, and I felt thoroughly inadequate in my ability to converse with God. Through spiritual direction with a Franciscan monk, I learned my own natural way of speaking to God was actually prayer.

Where was Barefoot Crossing when I needed it?!

Barefoot Crossing is indeed a "take off your sandals in the presence of God" holy space. But it's a holy space filled with a God that laughs with delight that we are together and able to say what we want, knowing that nothing we say will move God away from us.

These readings are very real, very present, relational conversations with God. "Dear God what did you do today?" "Lord of our laundromat." "Oh, hi! How long have you been here?" In their complete trust of God's faithfulness, the conversations can be tough. "We were serious about needing a definition of 'neighbor.' We really want to know what neighbors we can ignore and still pass the course."

Barefoot Crossing is for those who see the world in its complexities and want to lift concerns to God and for those who want God sitting on your bedroom floor giggling with you over your day. Deb invites us not just to read, but to engage with one another in the comments and create our own holy space of speaking and listening in human community.

Pastor Cindy Beck

Sierra Pacific Synod of ELCA

Introduction

Why did I write Barefoot Crossing?

- The name is sparked by the burning bush in the Bible's book of Exodus. God spoke to Moses out of that bush. Acknowledging the holy ground, Moses took off his sandals and stood barefooted. The conversation was intimate and honest.
- Scripture reading is one way I believe God speaks. Anyone can read scripture and start a conversation. The Bible is not a magical book. It does not require an academic degree or ordination papers.
- I read a few selected verses of scripture and had a barefooted, authentic conversation with whatever captured my attention. Barefoot Crossing seemed like a good name. The logo on the book cover is my artistic version of burning bush encounter.

How to read Barefoot Crossing

- Any way you want. I hope this will be a spark for your own encounter. There is no particular order. Each scripture verse and related prayer stands on its own.
- The scripture verses for each conversation are printed for you to read with space for your own barefooted conversation.

- The prayer includes the snippet of verse that caught my attention that day.

Why Barefoot Crossing matters?

- I am most grateful, most alive, most at home inside my own skin when I have had these barefooted and honest conversations.
- If God can speak through a burning bush, God can speak through ancient witnesses and people today including you and me. I pray the sparks from these encounters will light your space.
- This is holy ground. Bare feet are welcome.

Thankful for...

- The readers of barefootcrossing.substack.com who offer their conversation and encouragement.
- Donations received through Jazzwater.com to help me continue to share my words and art for the greater good.
- Cindy Beck. Your encouragement, and conversations have helped this book happen.

-debgrant

holy ground
barefeet welcome

✳ 1 ✳

Jeremiah 51:47-50

Assuredly, the days are coming when I will
punish the images of Babylon; her whole land
shall be put to shame, and all her slain shall
fall in her midst. Then the heavens and the
earth, and all that is in them, shall shout for
joy over Babylon; for the destroyers shall come
against them out of the north, says the LORD.
Babylon must fall for the slain of Israel, as the
slain of all the earth have fallen because of
Babylon. You survivors of the sword, go, do
not linger! Remember the LORD in a distant
land, and let Jerusalem come into your mind.

※ 1 ※
· · · · · · · · · · ·

"Remember the Lord in a distant land..."

God of Geography,
You have plotted our movements.
Watched us wander.
Chose when to follow us closely or at a distance.
Sometimes you stand at intersections
and wait for a drive-by sighting.
Find us today at this crossing place.
We will take off our shoes.
We will wiggle our toes.
We will wait and listen.
Point at your map, God, and tell us,
"You, child, are here."
Tell us you are too.
Remove the distance between us
as only you can.
Amen

✖ 2 ✖

Zechariah 14:10-11

The whole land shall be turned into a plain
from Geba to Rimmon south of Jerusalem. But
Jerusalem shall remain aloft on its site from the
Gate of Benjamin to the place of the former
gate, to the Corner Gate, and from the Tower of
Hananel to the king's wine presses. And it shall
be inhabited, for never again shall it be doomed
to destruction; Jerusalem shall abide in security.

✴ 2 ✴

. . . .

**"...and from the Tower of Hananel
to the King's winepresses."**

God of those who've lost their GPS,
you are the one leaning on a chair
waiting outside a roadside store
waiting for a conversation or a question.
We are travelers waiting for the courage
to admit we need help.
Tell us, friend, where are we?
How do we get to some place safe?
How do we get home?
You give us landmarks and city limits.
We can trust you. You are one of the locals.
The kind that has mercy.
Amen.

✳ 3 ✳

Luke 10:1-5

After this the Lord appointed seventy others and sent them on ahead of him in pairs to every town and place where he himself intended to go. He said to them, 'The harvest is plentiful, but the laborers are few; therefore ask the Lord of the harvest to send out laborers into his harvest. Go on your way. See, I am sending you out like lambs into the midst of wolves. Carry no purse, no bag, no sandals; and greet no one on the road. Whatever house you enter, first say, "Peace to this house!"

※ 3 ※

"Carry no purse, no bag, no sandals..."

Our Transportation Security Admin,
Our gate check agent, you limit our luggage.
You unburden our bags.
You focus us on our destination.
Lighten the load of our fear of scarcity.
Help us to trust your generosity.
Free us from distractions
to love the ones who are
each day's final destination.
Amen

✳ 4 ✳

Thomas said to him, 'Lord, we do not know where you are going. How can we know the way?' Jesus said to him, 'I am the way, and the truth, and the life. No one comes to the Father except through me. If you know me, you will know my Father also. From now on you do know him and have seen him.'

※ 4 ※

"...you do know him and have seen him."

God of All the Descendants of Uncertainty,
you are still here.
You have not lost patience
with generations of doubters and despair.
Stack a stone.
Bend a branch.
Drop a crumb.
We cannot see the future,
only the hint of how to follow you,
only the next step.
Left foot. Right foot. Left foot. Right foot.
Thanks for not walking too fast.
Amen

✳ 5 ✳

Jeremiah 8:4-6

You shall say to them, Thus says the Lord:
When people fall, do they not get up again?
If they go astray, do they not turn back? Why
then has this people turned away in perpetual
backsliding? They have held fast to deceit, they
have refused to return. I have given heed and
listened, but they do not speak honestly; no
one repents of wickedness, saying, 'What have
I done!' All of them turn to their own course,
like a horse plunging headlong into battle.

✳ 5 ✳

"...they have refused to return."

Oh, One who never gives up
on those
too stubborn
or too tired
or too ashamed
to stretch arms up with empty
hands and pleading fingers.
We need help.
We will try again.
We need to reach into your supply of do-overs.
Perfection is not the goal.
Closeness is.
So thank you for staying within arm's reach.
Amen

※ 6 ※
· · · · · · · · · · · ·

Joshua 23:1-5

A long time afterwards, when the Lord had given
rest to Israel from all their enemies all around,
and Joshua was old and well advanced in years,
Joshua summoned all Israel, their elders and
heads, their judges and officers, and said to them,
'I am now old and well advanced in years; and
you have seen all that the Lord your God has
done to all these nations for your sake, for it is
the Lord your God who has fought for you. I
have allotted to you as an inheritance for your
tribes those nations that remain, along with all
the nations that I have already cut off, from the
Jordan to the Great Sea in the west. The Lord
your God will push them back before you, and
drive them out of your sight; and you shall possess
their land, as the Lord your God promised you.

※ 6 ※

"I have allotted to you as an inheritance..."

God of Our Will and Testament,
you have given us this life to live,
this land to tend,
these days in which to know work and laughter.
Embedded in our chest is the capacity
to receive love and to give it.
The baton to be passed is filled with light,
not a burden but the best of the best
for the rest that come after us.
To those we love we put love in their hands.
To those we love we put their hands in yours.
Amen

✻ 7 ✻

Psalm 25:1-5

To you, O Lord, I lift up my soul. O my God, in you I trust; do not let me be put to shame; do not let my enemies exult over me. Do not let those who wait for you be put to shame; let them be ashamed who are wantonly treacherous. Make me to know your ways, O Lord; teach me your paths. Lead me in your truth, and teach me, for you are the God of my salvation; for you I wait all day long.

✳ 7 ✳
·············

"For you I wait all day long..."

God of Our Noisy Stomach Waiting,
receive our empty bowl,
our begging bowl.
We have eaten our fill
of our own heartburn.
We taste
the reflux of the past
we never learned from.
Calm and soothe us,
O God of guts and grace.
Save us from the inside out.
Amen.

※ 8 ※

Genesis 41:46-49

Joseph was thirty years old when he entered the service of Pharaoh king of Egypt. And Joseph went out from the presence of Pharaoh, and went through all the land of Egypt. During the seven plenteous years the earth produced abundantly. He gathered up all the food of the seven years when there was plenty in the land of Egypt, and stored up food in the cities; he stored up in every city the food from the fields around it. So Joseph stored up grain in such abundance—like the sand of the sea—that he stopped measuring it; it was beyond measure.

☀ 8 ☀
· · · · · · · · · · · ·

"the earth produced abundantly"

God of Inconsistent Weather,
of downpour and drought,
and yes, feast and famine.
Scarcity terrifies us.
Abundance makes us short-sighted.
Power is grabbed and horded
by those who bet the future.
Grant us the wisdom to save for rainy days
and still enjoy our days.
May we be generous
no matter what
the weather brings.
Amen

✗ 9 ✗

Leviticus 19:32-34

You shall rise before the aged, and defer to the old; and you shall fear your God: I am the Lord. When an alien resides with you in your land, you shall not oppress the alien. The alien who resides with you shall be to you as the citizen among you; you shall love the alien as yourself, for you were aliens in the land of Egypt: I am the Lord your God.

✖ 9 ✖
. . . .

"You shall love the alien as yourself."

Guardian Teacher
of our generation's short-term memory,
you slap sticky notes on bathroom mirrors
to remind us of who we are,
where we have been,
why we are here.
Put a piece of chalk in our hands,
if necessary,
have us stay after school.
Let our chalk board say:
You shall love the alien as yourself,
You shall love the alien as yourself,
You shall love the alien as yourself.
We don't own the land.
We are here to love on it.
Amen.

✳ 10 ✳
. . . .

Luke 10:33-37

But a Samaritan while travelling came near him;
and when he saw him, he was moved with pity.
He went to him and bandaged his wounds,
having poured oil and wine on them. Then he
put him on his own animal, brought him to an
inn, and took care of him. The next day he took
out two denarii, gave them to the innkeeper,
and said, "Take care of him; and when I come
back, I will repay you whatever more you spend."
Which of these three, do you think, was a
neighbor to the man who fell into the hands of
the robbers?' He said, 'The one who showed him
mercy.' Jesus said to him, 'Go and do likewise.'

✳ 10 ✳
. . . .

"Go and do likewise."

Have pity, Teacher, on us.
Is this on the syllabus? Will there be a quiz?
My dog ate the parable.
We were serious about needing
a definition of neighbor.
We really want to know what neighbors
we can ignore and still pass the course.
You pointed to a stranger in need and
you followed up with one least-likely-
to-be-our-choice of role model.
And then, (here's the real kicker)
you believed in us.
You believe that we too could see our neighbor's
need, act, have pity and show mercy.
Good and tough teachers believe in their students.
You, Holy Teach, rock good and tough.
Amen.

※ 11 ※

Psalm 25:16-20

Turn to me and be gracious to me, for I am lonely and afflicted. Relieve the troubles of my heart, and bring me out of my distress. Consider my affliction and my trouble, and forgive all my sins. Consider how many are my foes, and with what violent hatred they hate me. O guard my life, and deliver me; do not let me be put to shame, for I take refuge in you.

☀ 11 ☀
· · · · · · · · · · · ·

"Turn to me and be gracious to me..."

God of I and Me and Mine,
you hear our cries and whines
from within our dark rooms
and behind the cringing lids of eyes.
You listen to our loneliness
and our woeful list of This is Awful.
While we are crying, you multi-task.
You listen and gift wrap.
You wrap our lives in your eternal yes
and reach into our darkness,
re-light the pilot light,
and give us sight again.
Again you say,
"Look, this is for you. this is for you."
Amen.

✳ 12 ✳

Proverbs 19:15-17

Laziness brings on deep sleep; an idle person will
suffer hunger. Those who keep the commandment
will live; those who are heedless of their ways
will die. Whoever is kind to the poor lends
to the LORD, and will be repaid in full.

✻ 12 ✻
. . . .

**"...those who are heedless of
their ways will die."**

Oh, My God of Look at What You are Doing!
You long for us
to be self-aware,
to be with humility,
without arrogance,
without ignoring everyone around us.
Show us, O God, how to heed our ways.
May we see those in need before us
and those tumbling in our wake behind us.
May we pay attention to those walking with us.
Heeder of our lives,
thank you for another day to pay attention.
Amen

✳ 13 ✳

Ecclesiastes. 9:14-18

There was a little city with few people in it. A great
king came against it and besieged it, building great
siege-works against it. Now there was found in it
a poor, wise man, and he by his wisdom delivered
the city. Yet no one remembered that poor man.
So I said, 'Wisdom is better than might; yet the
poor man's wisdom is despised, and his words
are not heeded.' The quiet words of the wise are
more to be heeded than the shouting of a ruler
among fools. Wisdom is better than weapons
of war, but one bungler destroys much good.

✻ 13 ✻
· · · · · · · · · · · ·

"...one bungler destroys much good"

God of War, you are no fool.
You know well how we fight and fortress.
We know too well how
to arm ourselves for battle.
We wield weapons and words
of mass destruction.
We design the finest swords
to put in the hands of fools.
Send us back to school.
Show us how to pick a good fight
and brandish wisdom.
May we be alive to celebrate
the end of war even with the fools.
Amen

✲ 14 ✲

O Lord, who may abide in your tent? Who may dwell on your holy hill? Those who walk blamelessly, and do what is right, and speak the truth from their heart; who do not slander with their tongue, and do no evil to their friends, nor take up a reproach against their neighbors; in whose eyes the wicked are despised, but who honor those who fear the Lord; who stand by their oath even to their hurt; who do not lend money at interest, and do not take a bribe against the innocent. Those who do these things shall never be moved.

※ 14 ※

"who may abide in your tent?"

Tent Pitcher,
Your tent. Your rules. Seems fair.
Until we want our freedom
more than the belonging space
under the stars in your backyard.
Your voice. Your stories.
Your face half-visible in the flashlight
and half a mystery.
Your tent. Your rules.
Family. Friends. Neighbors.
We have no room in here for lies.
No matter what the night brings,
we breath the air of home.
Amen

✳ 15 ✳

Ephesians 3:14-19

For this reason I bow my knees before the Father, from whom every family in heaven and on earth takes its name. I pray that, according to the riches of his glory, he may grant that you may be strengthened in your inner being with power through his Spirit, and that Christ may dwell in your hearts through faith, as you are being rooted and grounded in love. I pray that you may have the power to comprehend, with all the saints, what is the breadth and length and height and depth, and to know the love of Christ that surpasses knowledge, so that you may be filled with all the fullness of God.

✳ 15 ✳

"so that you may be filled with the fullness of God."

God of Full Service, fill'er up.
Give us the good stuff.
The high octane. The premium.
We acknowledge our emptiness.
Our hollow days.
Our need for power beyond our grasp.
Our sputtering fumes to get by from day to day.
You, God, are more than pit stop.
You are
the vehicle, the road, the fuel,
the driver, the passenger.
Fill us up with you.
Amen

✳ 16 ✳

Genesis 14:14-16

When Abram heard that his nephew had been taken captive, he led forth his trained men, born in his house, three hundred and eighteen of them, and went in pursuit as far as Dan. He divided his forces against them by night, he and his servants, and routed them and pursued them to Hobah, north of Damascus. Then he brought back all the goods, and also brought back his nephew Lot with his goods, and the women and the people.

✳ 16 ✳

"his nephew had been taken captive..."

Oh, Abram, trail blazer of your family's
far-reaching faith,
you took care of family.
You brought back the goods,
the nephew,
the nephew's goods,
the women
and the people.
We'd like to believe that this list
isn't in order of priority.
We'll give you the benefit of the doubt about
your favorites in this messy forming family.
You were still learning about the grace
that pulses through this blood line.
So are we.
We are still learning, still trusting.
You 'brought back all.' That sounds right.
Instead of picking favorites, bring back all.
Amen

※ 17 ※

Luke 10:38-42

Now as they went on their way, he entered a certain village, where a woman named Martha welcomed him into her home. She had a sister named Mary, who sat at the Lord's feet and listened to what he was saying. But Martha was distracted by her many tasks; so she came to him and asked, 'Lord, do you not care that my sister has left me to do all the work by myself? Tell her then to help me.' But the Lord answered her, 'Martha, Martha, you are worried and distracted by many things; there is need of only one thing. Mary has chosen the better part, which will not be taken away from her.'

※ 17 ※

"Martha, Martha, you are worried and distracted by many things."

Jesus,
we welcome you like Martha.
We try to listen to you like Mary,
but then there are chores, to-do lists,
must-do, should do, and the voice in our
heads and puffing out our face saying,
"Can we get some help in here?"
The to-do lists happen in due time
and never end.
Our pleas for help happen and never end.
In between the din of voices, there is yours.
There is always yours.
Speak our name through the noise.
Our ears perk to our name
sung in the sound of you.
Say it twice if you have to.
Amen.

✳ 18 ✳
. . . .

Psalm 119:97-98, 103-104

Oh, how I love your law! It is my meditation all day long. Your commandment makes me wiser than my enemies, for it is always with me. How sweet are your words to my taste, sweeter than honey to my mouth! Through your precepts I get understanding; therefore I hate every false way.

✳ 18 ✳
. . . .

"...sweet are your words to my taste."

God, our taste bud,
your salivary wisdom comes to us
like a smorgasbord, a buffet,
a deliciously lucky potluck.
Everyone gets to choose a morsel.
Not all of us choose wisely.
Educate our palates
with ingredients of truth we can trust
from the hands of cooks who care.
May what we choose to take in
truly nurture a body of compassion.
Amen

✳ 19 ✳

I John 2:1-6

My little children, I am writing these things to you
so that you may not sin. But if anyone does sin,
we have an advocate with the Father, Jesus Christ
the righteous; and he is the atoning sacrifice for
our sins, and not for ours only but also for the sins
of the whole world. Now by this we may be sure
that we know him if we obey his commandments.
Whoever says, 'I have come to know him', but
does not obey his commandments, is a liar, and
in such a person the truth does not exist; but
whoever obeys his word, truly in this person the
love of God has reached perfection. By this we
may be sure that we are in him: whoever says, 'I
abide in him', ought to walk just as he walked.

✳ 19 ✳
. . . .

"I abide in him."

Son of God, Walking Man, you walked
everywhere through towns, to crowds, to
hurting ones. You rode a time or two by boat
and once by donkey, but mostly you walked.
We walk along but we are still
trying to keep up the pace
while listening, watching, learning.
You match our stride more often
than we match yours.
You love the world you are walking in,
and the people you are walking with,
the people who are blistered and
tired, thirsty and hungry,
the people who have what others
need along the way and have not yet
learned to give themselves away,
and the more we walk with you, we get that.
Amen

✳ 20 ✳
· · · · · · · · · · · · · · ·

John 6:47-51

Very truly, I tell you, whoever believes has eternal life. I am the bread of life. Your ancestors ate the manna in the wilderness, and they died. This is the bread that comes down from heaven, so that one may eat of it and not die. I am the living bread that came down from heaven. Whoever eats of this bread will live forever; and the bread that I will give for the life of the world is my flesh.'

✕ 20 ✕

**"...the bread I will give for
the life of the world..."**

God of the Hungry,
of fast food and takeout,
of leftovers, and skipped lunches,
of we can't remember what we ate this morning,
of hamburger that needs help
and fries that come with that,
of have you seen the price of groceries?
and how do people with kids get by?
May we take you in. Eat you up.
May we become what we eat.
May we become grateful.
May we become what is needed
for the hungry to make it to another day.
May we become "here, take my sandwich."
Amen

✳ **21** ✳
. . . .

Psalm 138:4-8

All the kings of the earth shall praise you, O Lord, for they have heard the words of your mouth. They shall sing of the ways of the Lord, for great is the glory of the Lord. For though the Lord is high, he regards the lowly; but the haughty he perceives from far away. Though I walk in the midst of trouble, you preserve me against the wrath of my enemies; you stretch out your hand, and your right hand delivers me. The Lord will fulfil his purpose for me; your steadfast love, O Lord, endures forever. Do not forsake the work of your hands.

※ 21 ※

"though I walk in the most of trouble..."

Holy God of Here Comes Trouble,
Into the thick of it,
up to your armpits,
you wade in.
You reach out.
We thrash around and make things worse.
Panic or despair sets in while we sink deeper.
Your hand is there.
Open.
Ready.
Reaching.
Our hands work the same way.
Help us to remember that
when someone's sinking.
Amen

✳ 22 ✳
. . . .

John 20:15-18

Jesus said to her, 'Woman, why are you weeping?
For whom are you looking?' Supposing him to
be the gardener, she said to him, 'Sir, if you have
carried him away, tell me where you have laid
him, and I will take him away.' Jesus said to her,
'Mary!' She turned and said to him in Hebrew,
'Rabboni!' (which means Teacher). Jesus said
to her, 'Do not hold on to me, because I have
not yet ascended to the Father. But go to my
brothers and say to them, "I am ascending to
my Father and your Father, to my God and your
God." ' Mary Magdalene went and announced
to the disciples, 'I have seen the Lord'; and she
told them that he had said these things to her.

✳ **22** ✳

"I have seen the Lord."

O Mary, don't you weep. Don't you mourn.
You rushed through leaden days to be a leader.
Your unrestrained voice
broke through your brothers' stubborn
'I have to see him for myself.'
Your joy scrambled through centuries
of the debris of your unfairly sullied reputation.
We hear your clarion song, O Easter Sister.
Lead us to see that
splendid morning rise
in our stubborn eyes.
Teach us the melody and the lyrics
of your unsullied song of truth.
Amen

✳ 23 ✳
· · · · · · · · · · · · · ·

Then Esther said in reply to Mordecai, 'Go,
gather all the Jews to be found in Susa, and hold
a fast on my behalf, and neither eat nor drink
for three days, night or day. I and my maids
will also fast as you do. After that I will go to
the king, though it is against the law; and if I
perish, I perish.' Mordecai then went away and
did everything as Esther had ordered him.

✳ 23 ✳

"...I will go to the king, though it is against the law."

God of this courageous woman,
you wove her together
with wisdom and guts.
Our bravery without clarity spins without thread.
When we are full of ourselves,
our calls to action unwind.
May we think beyond ourselves and listen.
Gather us as brave fibers
entwined with courage
laced with wisdom
and a will to weave justice.
Amen

✳ 24 ✳

Luke 11:1-4

He was praying in a certain place, and after he had finished, one of his disciples said to him, 'Lord, teach us to pray, as John taught his disciples.' He said to them, 'When you pray, say: Father, hallowed be your name. Your kingdom come. Give us each day our daily bread. And forgive us our sins, for we ourselves forgive everyone indebted to us. And do not bring us to the time of trial.'

☼ 24 ☼
. . . .

Lord, teach us to pray..."

Primer of the Prayer Pump, you gave us words.
Holy Name. Dream Home. Dinner's
Ready. Grace Always.
Your words to pull our words
from the deep well of our wanting
to talk with you.
Our words can't reach the surface without help.
We want answers.
You want us. All of us. All our words.
The stomach-churning words of
questions, abandonment, and fear.
Holy Name. Dream Home. Dinner's
Ready. Grace Always.
Thank you for the words
when we don't know what to say
but we know we want to say our words
to you.
Amen

✳ 25 ✳

Mark 10:35-40

James and John, the sons of Zebedee, came
forward to him and said to him, 'Teacher, we want
you to do for us whatever we ask of you.' And he
said to them, 'What is it you want me to do for
you?' And they said to him, 'Grant us to sit, one
at your right hand and one at your left, in your
glory.' But Jesus said to them, 'You do not know
what you are asking. Are you able to drink the cup
that I drink, or be baptized with the baptism that
I am baptized with?' They replied, 'We are able.'
Then Jesus said to them, 'The cup that I drink
you will drink; and with the baptism with which
I am baptized, you will be baptized; but to sit at
my right hand or at my left is not mine to grant,
but it is for those for whom it has been prepared.'

✳ 25 ✳
. . . .

"Teacher, we want you to do for us whatever we ask of you."

Dear Mark,

We are writing to tell you that we love your book. You write with such precision. No flowery rhetoric that boasts of a vocabulary bigger than us. Crisp sentence structure. Minimalist detail. We appreciate your strategic placement of events in the narrative.

But mostly, Mark, (may we call you Mark?) you gave us a picture - no, more than that - you wrote us into the story so that we could experience being taught by Jesus in person. And face to face, we feel the boldness of the familiarity with Jesus to ask any question and the shame of asking for favors that miss the point. Love your work.

Best Regards.

Amen

✳ 26 ✳

Romans 10:1-4

Brothers and sisters, my heart's desire and prayer to God for them is that they may be saved. I can testify that they have a zeal for God, but it is not enlightened. For, being ignorant of the righteousness that comes from God, and seeking to establish their own, they have not submitted to God's righteousness. For Christ is the end of the law so that there may be righteousness for everyone who believes.

❊ 26 ❊
. . . .

"...being ignorant of the righteousness of God."

God of Righteousness,
is there a wrong-teousness? Asking for a friend.
We have a feeling that this life with you
was not intended to be theology.
An intellectual exercise. A seminar.
A doctoral thesis defense.
Or worse, a plot to keep most of us ashamed
of what we don't know.
Forgive us for the flotsam and jetsam
of our vocabulary.
Would it help to know that we don't
know how to describe you?
The messy stuff we understand.
It's the grace that blows us away.
Amen

※ 27 ※
....

Matthew 5:43-48

You have heard that it was said, "You shall love your neighbor and hate your enemy." But I say to you, Love your enemies and pray for those who persecute you, so that you may be children of your Father in heaven; for he makes his sun rise on the evil and on the good, and sends rain on the righteous and on the unrighteous. For if you love those who love you, what reward do you have? Do not even the tax-collectors do the same? And if you greet only your brothers and sisters, what more are you doing than others? Do not even the Gentiles do the same? Be perfect, therefore, as your heavenly Father is perfect.

✳ 27 ✳

**"You have heard that it was
said...but I say to you..."**

Jesus, could you make it more difficult?
You want us to flip the script.
Turn inside out. Upside down.
Our familiar instinct of tit for tat, all's fair,
even up the score is what we know.
It is the way the world works.
Yes, it is a bitter, never-ending loop.
What you are asking changes the game.
It could change the world within our reach.
Love first. Love first.
Some of us have little experience with love.
You are asking us to love big
when we have been loved little.
To love when we ache to be loved.
To love when it is difficult.
Give us time to practice.
We'll try. Please don't give up.
Amen.

✳ 28 ✳

Why should I fear in times of trouble, when
the iniquity of my persecutors surrounds me,
those who trust in their wealth and boast
of the abundance of their riches? Truly, no
ransom avails for one's life, there is no price
one can give to God for it. For the ransom of
life is costly, and can never suffice, that one
should live on forever and never see the grave.

※ 28 ※

"There is no price one can give to God..."

O God, Tipper of the Scales,
our worth is measured
not by the time in our lives,
not by the length of our resume,
not by anything we measure.
We are yours.
We are priceless.
May the time and gifts leased to us in this life
be used to enjoy your grace
and to have more parties
than we can count.
Amen

※ **29** ※
. . . .

Proverbs 24:1-4

Do not envy the wicked, nor desire to be
with them; for their minds devise violence,
and their lips talk of mischief. By wisdom
a house is built, and by understanding it
is established; by knowledge the rooms are
filled with all precious and pleasant riches.

✳ **29** ✳
. . . .

"By wisdom a house is built...by knowledge the rooms are filled..."

Architect and Contractor God,
you lay our foundation.
You create the pattern
of our comings and goings,
the movement of our daily light and shadows,
windows and doors that open and close.
We are free to choose our interior design
with thoughtfulness or cruelty,
understanding or selfishness.
May we be a dwelling place with doors t
hat swing open often,
A house with plenty of unclaimed rooms
and extra spaces at our tables.
Amen

✳ 30 ✳

Ecclesiastes 1:9-11

What has been is what will be, and what has been done is what will be done; there is nothing new under the sun. Is there a thing of which it is said, 'See, this is new'? It has already been, in the ages before us. The people of long ago are not remembered, nor will there be any remembrance of people yet to come by those who come after them.

✳ 30 ✳

"Nothing new under the sun."

God of the Script,
you have seen this plot before,
this story line, these characters.
You have seen it all
despite our best efforts
to re-invent the trajectory of our history.
Our lives are short.
Our memories shorter.
We seemed doomed to repeat the failures.
And yet, here we are, God,
just grateful to have a part.
May the sun shine on our time today
on the stage
and find love stealing the spotlight
for a change.
Amen

✳ 31 ✳

Luke 12:16-21

Then he told them a parable: 'The land of a rich man produced abundantly. And he thought to himself, "What should I do, for I have no place to store my crops?" Then he said, "I will do this: I will pull down my barns and build larger ones, and there I will store all my grain and my goods. And I will say to my soul, Soul, you have ample goods laid up for many years; relax, eat, drink, be merry." But God said to him, "You fool! This very night your life is being demanded of you. And the things you have prepared, whose will they be?" So it is with those who store up treasures for themselves but are not rich towards God.'

✳ 31 ✳

"I will store all my grain and my goods..."

Jesus, what a parable.
Our storage units are filled with
mine and my and maybe we
will need this someday.
Our fears empty store shelves.
Help us loosen our hording grip
and put us within arm's reach
of who is important.
Flex the muscle of our heart to roar
with the courage to remember who you are
and who we are
and what we never stand to lose
because you gave us everything.
We have everything we need
to live generously.
Amen

✳ 32 ✳

Psalm 127:1-2

Unless the Lord builds the house, those who build it labor in vain. Unless the Lord guards the city, the guard keeps watch in vain. It is in vain that you rise up early and go late to rest, eating the bread of anxious toil; for he gives sleep to his beloved.

✳ 32 ✳

"for he gives sleep to his beloved."

God of the Wee Hours,
we lay sandwiched between twisted sheets
and video replays of our days.
Our plans and our fears
buzz and land,
buzz and land.
Little night bandits stealing our sleep,
our time to heal, to rest, to hope,
to dream perchance to build
and guard what is ours together.
Show us how to trust you
with our lives and loves.
Gift us with blessed sleep
And a new day.
Amen.

✵ 33 ✵

Colossians 4:2-6

Devote yourselves to prayer, keeping alert in
it with thanksgiving. At the same time pray
for us as well that God will open to us a door
for the word, that we may declare the mystery
of Christ, for which I am in prison, so that
I may reveal it clearly, as I should. Conduct
yourselves wisely towards outsiders, making
the most of the time. Let your speech always be
gracious, seasoned with salt, so that you may
know how you ought to answer everyone.

✳ **33** ✳
. . . .

"Let your speech always be gracious..."

Creator of the Human Larynx,
You gave us this body part with which
we gargle, breathe, swallow, give our
food a passing glance and talk.
It knows us well.
It knows our every spoken, shouted,
and whispered word.
We thank you for its practicality and power.
May we use it to exhale the arrogance
of our puffery prayers.
May we use it to inhale wisdom,
To say we're sorry with sincerity.
May we use it to propel
the sounds of grace
into the cacophony of our space.
Amen

✳ 34 ✳

Ecclesiastes 12:13b-14

The end of the matter; all has been heard. Fear God, and keep his commandments; for that is the whole duty of everyone. For God will bring every deed into judgement, including every secret thing, whether good or evil.

✳ **34** ✳

**"...including every secret thing,
whether good or evil."**

To the One
who hears a bazillion prayers
that start with 'You know everything.'
Here we go again.
And because we have been here before
our fear of you is well-informed.
You know a lot about us.
We know less about you.
We don't know everything about you,
however, this we know:
We have known occasions in your presence
where we have forgiveness, justice and joy.
May we trust you with our secrets
so that our next steps together might be lighter,
so that we might be caught in the act
of being yours.
Amen

※ 35 ※

Psalm 33:20-22

Our soul waits for the Lord; he is our help and shield. Our heart is glad in him, because we trust in his holy name. Let your steadfast love, O Lord, be upon us, even as we hope in you.

❊ 35 ❊

"our heart is glad in God because we trust..."

Trustworthy One,
sometimes we can point to the past and see you.
You are the one who has kept your promises.
Most of the time we are stalled in the
present and fearful of the future.
Our faith is often tired resignation.
"You, Lord, you're the best we've got...
to whom shall we go?"
Not a great statement of faith,
but the best we can do most days.
We are tempted by those who offer empty
promises for our affection. But we are
tired of being scammed. So we wait.
Waiting sucks. (pardon my language, Lord)
BUT you are the real deal. We trust you.
But respectfully, you do steadfast
better than us.
Amen.

✳ **36** ✳
· · · · · · · · · · · · ·

Ecclesiastes. 6:1-2

There is an evil that I have seen under the
sun, and it lies heavy upon humankind: those
to whom God gives wealth, possessions, and
honor, so that they lack nothing of all that
they desire, yet God does not enable them
to enjoy these things, but a stranger enjoys
them. This is vanity; it is a grievous ill.

❊ 36 ❊

"it lies heavy upon humankind..."

Wisdom,
There is so much under the sun.
There is so much evil.
There is so little time.
There is too much for us to remember.
It is too much for a refrigerator
magnet to hold before our eyes.
Perhaps you can develop a creative way
to help us each day to confront the truth
about wealth and possessions and honor.
May we be wise enough, at least,
to remember that the gift is always a gift.
The way we live is our thank you note.
Amen

✳ **37** ✳

Matthew 6:19-21

'Do not store up for yourselves treasures on earth, where moth and rust consume and where thieves break in and steal; but store up for yourselves treasures in heaven, where neither moth nor rust consumes and where thieves do not break in and steal. For where your treasure is, there your heart will be also.

✳ 37 ✳
. . . .

**"For where your treasure is, there
your heart will be also."**

Precious,
we know the difference between rust and gold.
We understand the hands that fight
and the hands that hold.
We know you love us without being told
and yet....
and yet...
the telling and retelling is never wasted time.
Tell us again about the day we were born.
Amen

※ 38 ※

'Do not be afraid, little flock, for it is your Father's good pleasure to give you the kingdom. Sell your possessions, and give alms. Make purses for yourselves that do not wear out, an unfailing treasure in heaven, where no thief comes near and no moth destroys. For where your treasure is, there your heart will be also.

※ 38 ※

"Do not be afraid, little flock."

But Jesus, we are afraid.
We are separated from the others.
We are not one, big, happy family.
We are not one with you as you are one.
We are afraid of the other little flocks,
the thieves in the night.
Not to mention the pesky moths.
Our fear is what makes us so little.
Too small to live. Too small to give.
Shove our little hearts into your deep pockets.
Let us rest awhile in your care
so that we might find the courage
to love beyond our size of our fear.
Amen

✳ **39** ✳
. . . .

Psalm 89:1-4

I will sing of your steadfast love, O Lord, forever; with my mouth I will proclaim your faithfulness to all generations. I declare that your steadfast love is established for ever; your faithfulness is as firm as the heavens. You said, 'I have made a covenant with my chosen one, I have sworn to my servant David: "I will establish your descendants for ever, and build your throne for all generations."

✳ **39** ✳
·············

"I will sing of your steadfast love"

God who is in the House,
Front row center. Ready to listen, to applaud,
to wish us "break a leg" along with the
best of all who have ever sung for you.
All your children have a place in the choir.
Some can't sing or carry a tune.
Some come because their spouse made them or
bribed them with a restaurant lunch afterwards.
So here we are with an audience of One
to sing a love song
because no one knows how messy we are
better than you.
No one keeps humming in our ears
through the years like you.
You deserve a song.
Even a half-hearted attempt will have to do.
And because of you, it will.
And because of that we keep on singing.
Amen

✳ 40 ✳

Hebrews 11:17-19

By faith Abraham, when put to the test, offered up Isaac. He who had received the promises was ready to offer up his only son, of whom he had been told, 'It is through Isaac that descendants shall be named after you.' He considered the fact that God is able even to raise someone from the dead—and figuratively speaking, he did receive him back.

※ 40 ※

"...descendants shall be named for you."

Isaac,
you were old enough to see
your father's anguish and his knife.
You were old enough to be confused.
Centuries later we confess we are confused too.
We are confused by God's instruction.
Abraham's obedience.
The idea of a test of faith leaves us hollow
in the middle of so many voices convinced
they know what God was thinking.
All we know for certain is that you, Isaac,
whose name means laughter
had a long life after with your own kids.
May it be enough to believe
through our confusion
even as you did.
Amen

✳ 41 ✳
. . . .

Luke 12: 41-44

Peter said, 'Lord, are you telling this parable for
us or for everyone?' And the Lord said, 'Who
then is the faithful and prudent manager whom
his master will put in charge of his slaves, to give
them their allowance of food at the proper time?
Blessed is that slave whom his master will find
at work when he arrives. Truly I tell you, he will
put that one in charge of all his possessions.

✳ 41 ✳

**"Peter said, 'Lord are you telling
this parable for us..."**

God of Peter,
What Peter said.
We don't understand either.
We squint. We stand on our heads.
We look sideways. We wonder if there is
a decoder ring. Do we have to know the
ancient languages. Is this one of those times
when we just have to have been there?
Slavery is wrong no matter the time in history.
It is hard for us to wring the
goodness out of this parable.
Maybe we are overthinking it.
Maybe it is about having integrity
and compassion in our work.
You didn't give up on Peter when he
didn't understand. We know you'll be
patient with us while we ponder.
Amen

✴ 42 ✴

Psalm 82: 1-4, 8

God has taken his place in the divine council; in
the midst of the gods he holds judgement: 'How
long will you judge unjustly and show partiality
to the wicked? Give justice to the weak and the
orphan; maintain the right of the lowly and
the destitute. Rescue the weak and the needy;
deliver them from the hand of the wicked.'
Rise up, O God, judge the earth; for
all the nations belong to you!

※ 42 ※
· · · · · · · · · · · · ·

"Deliver them from the hand of the wicked."

Jesus,
no one knows the vulnerability
of this bag of human flesh better than you.
You have known weakness, abandonment,
and unfair judgement.
There are always poor. You said that.
There are always people who are
lacking something.
There are always some who would
rather be cruel than just.
Give us courage to take a punch.
We know what it means to need a
champion from time to time.
There will always be someone who needs one.
Help us to be someone's champion
from time to time.
Amen

☀ **43** ☀
· · · · · · · · · · · · · ·

Hebrews 10:32-36

But recall those earlier days when, after you had been enlightened, you endured a hard struggle with sufferings, sometimes being publicly exposed to abuse and persecution, and sometimes being partners with those so treated. For you had compassion for those who were in prison, and you cheerfully accepted the plundering of your possessions, knowing that you yourselves possessed something better and more lasting. Do not, therefore, abandon that confidence of yours; it brings a great reward. For you need endurance, so that when you have done the will of God, you may receive what was promised.

✳ **43** ✳
. . . .

**"But recall those earlier days when...
you endured a hard struggle..."**

Time-Traveler and Band-aid Ripper,
The good old days are good because
we've healed of the not-so-good.
We forget the pain sometimes
and even the miracle of our scars.
Struggle is not new.
Grief is always with us.
What is new is us.
Each day,
wounded and healing,
grieving and celebrating.
We are still here.
You are too.
Amen

※ 44 ※

I Samuel 6:13-16

Now the people of Beth-shemesh were reaping
their wheat harvest in the valley. When they looked
up and saw the ark, they went with rejoicing to
meet it. The cart came into the field of Joshua of
Beth-shemesh, and stopped there. A large stone
was there; so they split up the wood of the cart
and offered the cows as a burnt offering to the
Lord. The Levites took down the ark of the Lord
and the box that was beside it, in which were the
gold objects, and set them upon the large stone.
Then the people of Beth-shemesh offered burnt-
offerings and presented sacrifices on that day to
the Lord. When the five lords of the Philistines
saw it, they returned that day to Ekron.

※ 44 ※
. . . .

"When they looked up and saw the ark..."

God of I AM,
Messenger who made us laugh,
Promiser of land and stars,
Covenant of word and stone,
Sender of reluctant prophets
and unprepared kings,
and Jesus of Follow Me.
We build altars and cathedrals,
icons and windows of colored shards
because sometimes we are just too little
and limited in our imagination
to love a God so big.
We keep finding galactic windows
with an even greater view.
So big,
we can't get over it.
Amen

✳ 45 ✳

'I came to bring fire to the earth, and how I
wish it were already kindled! I have a baptism
with which to be baptized, and what stress I
am under until it is completed! Do you think
that I have come to bring peace to the earth?
No, I tell you, but rather division! From now
on, five in one household will be divided, three
against two and two against three; they will be
divided: father against son and son against father,
mother against daughter and daughter against
mother, mother-in-law against her daughter-in-
law and daughter-in-law against mother-in-law.'

✳ 45 ✳
. . . .

"What stress I am under until it is completed"

Oh, God,
this is going to hurt.
Don't tell us it will get worse
before it gets better.
This is ugly enough already.
The fire is lit.
We are fighting among ourselves.
Inside our families. Inside ourselves.
What are we fighting about?
Who are we fighting for?
Tell us more about your stress and
what is this completion that you mention?
Right now, all that gives us hope
is that you understand stress
and that this won't last forever.
Amen

✳ **46** ✳
. . . .

And Mary said, 'My soul magnifies the Lord, and my spirit rejoices in God my Savior, for he has looked with favor on the lowliness of his servant. Surely, from now on all generations will call me blessed; for the Mighty One has done great things for me, and holy is his name.

✳ 46 ✳
. . . .

**"For he has looked with favor
on the lowliness..."**

Mary, girlfriend,
thank you for opening up your diary,
for giving us your unmuted moment
to hear the sound of the first disciple's faith.
Those who are acquainted with being disregarded
and dismissed
and told to be quiet
are grateful to be favored, heard and seen.
It happens so rarely your song resounds
through centuries of lowly souls.
May we magnify your love in our time
by amplifying the voices
who were taught only to whisper.
Amen

✳ **47** ✳

Acts 7:51-53

'You stiff-necked people, uncircumcised in heart and ears, you are forever opposing the Holy Spirit, just as your ancestors used to do. Which of the prophets did your ancestors not persecute? They killed those who foretold the coming of the Righteous One, and now you have become his betrayers and murderers. You are the ones that received the law as ordained by angels, and yet you have not kept it.'

※ 47 ※
. . . .

"You are the ones that received the law...and yet you have not kept it."

God of the stiff-necked,
the ones with stones in hand
who are more prepared to deal with the messenger
than the message.
And what about those of us in the cheap seats?
The ones sitting in the rarified air
above the drama while spectating.
The ones now armed with a click,
participating without participating.
God help us. God love us.
The law is heavier than stone and yet
never intended to be thrown
only to be owned
and carried by those who live to love.
By those who live to love.
Amen

✳ **48** ✳
. . . .

Jeremiah 25:34-38

Wail, you shepherds, and cry out; roll in ashes, you
lords of the flock, for the days of your slaughter
have come—and your dispersions, and you
shall fall like a choice vessel. Flight shall fail the
shepherds, and there shall be no escape for the
lords of the flock. Hark! the cry of the shepherds,
and the wail of the lords of the flock! For the
Lord is despoiling their pasture, and the peaceful
folds are devastated, because of the fierce anger
of the Lord. Like a lion he has left his covert;
for their land has become a waste because of the
cruel sword, and because of his fierce anger.

✳ **48** ✳

"Because of the fierce anger of the Lord..."

Angry God,
we pause before we miss the point
of Jeremiah's meltdown
and accuse you
of inconsistency (cough) hypocrisy
and push back with where does love and
patience fit with this temper tantrum?
We have a long history of knowing
what gets under your skin.
We can't claim ignorance.
You were serious when you said love.
Help us to love as fiercely.
Help us to take love as seriously
as you love us.
Amen

✳ **49** ✳
. . . .

Psalm 103:1-5

Bless the Lord, O my soul, and all that is within
me, bless his holy name. Bless the Lord, O my
soul, and do not forget all his benefits— who
forgives all your iniquity, who heals all your
diseases, who redeems your life from the Pit,
who crowns you with steadfast love and mercy,
who satisfies you with good as long as you live
so that your youth is renewed like the eagle's.

✖ 49 ✖

"who redeems your life from the pit..."

God of the ditch, the hole, the abyss,
we look up to find you.
We climb to summits to touch the air
where we believe you live with a view.
And then we come down.
Sometimes we plummet or stumble
or just let the darkness swallow us whole.
It is there where your presence is
less than fingerprint away.
Ready to teach us on the fly.
It is in the pit we discover you beneath us,
lifting us up for a better view.
Amen

※ 50 ※

2 Chronicles 8:12-15

Then Solomon offered up burnt-offerings to the
Lord on the altar of the Lord that he had built
in front of the vestibule, as the duty of each day
required, offering according to the commandment
of Moses for the sabbaths, the new moons,
and the three annual festivals—the festival of
unleavened bread, the festival of weeks, and the
festival of booths. According to the ordinance of
his father David, he appointed the divisions of
the priests for their service, and the Levites for
their offices of praise and ministry alongside the
priests as the duty of each day required, and the
gatekeepers in their divisions for the several gates;
for so David the man of God had commanded.
They did not turn away from what the king had
commanded the priests and Levites regarding
anything at all, or regarding the treasuries.

※ 50 ※

"...offerings for the sabbath, the new moons, and the three festivals..."

Everything is a season, a reason God,
you created the calendar of the moon and sun,
the people who noticed,
the stargazers who told kings,
the kings who built altars
to stand tippy-toe closer
to the sun and the moon and you.
You appointed servants to look up
to capture the attention of passing crowds
to make busy people pause,
stop in their tracks
and look up if only for a second
to say, 'Wow!'
Amen

☀ 51 ☀
. . . .

Nehemiah 13:19-22

When it began to be dark at the gates of Jerusalem
before the sabbath, I commanded that the doors
should be shut and gave orders that they should
not be opened until after the sabbath. And I set
some of my servants over the gates, to prevent any
burden from being brought in on the sabbath
day. Then the merchants and sellers of all kinds
of merchandise spent the night outside Jerusalem
once or twice. But I warned them and said to
them, 'Why do you spend the night in front of
the wall? If you do so again, I will lay hands on
you.' From that time on they did not come on the
sabbath. And I commanded the Levites that they
should purify themselves and come and guard the
gates, to keep the sabbath day holy. Remember
this also in my favor, O my God, and spare me
according to the greatness of your steadfast love.

✳ 51 ✳

"...to keep the sabbath day holy."

God of all that is holy,
when you declared sabbath,
we hear 'church attendance.'
You hear our excuses.
You hear us complain
about those who don't attend.
You keep the sabbath from our unholiness.
Every time we rest or pause or fall exhausted or
succumb to silence or remember what our lungs
can do...every time...you make that moment holy.
Every time you make that moment holy.
Every time
we learn there's more to learn about sabbath.
Amen

✳ 52 ✳

·············

Luke 13:11-16

And just then there appeared a woman with a
spirit that had crippled her for eighteen years. She
was bent over and was quite unable to stand up
straight. When Jesus saw her, he called her over and
said, 'Woman, you are set free from your ailment.'
When he laid his hands on her, immediately she
stood up straight and began praising God. But
the leader of the synagogue, indignant because
Jesus had cured on the sabbath, kept saying to the
crowd, 'There are six days on which work ought
to be done; come on those days and be cured, and
not on the sabbath day.' But the Lord answered
him and said, 'You hypocrites! Does not each of
you on the sabbath untie his ox or his donkey from
the manger, and lead it away to give it water? And
ought not this woman, a daughter of Abraham
whom Satan bound for eighteen long years, be
set free from this bondage on the sabbath day?'

✳ 52 ✳
· · · · · · · · · · · · ·

**"And ought not this woman...be set free
from this bondage on the sabbath day?"**

Holy God of hypocrites,
of inconsistency,
of what about,
of eyesight filled with lumber,
marinate our hard hearts in your grace.
Tenderize our cruelty
until we feel tenderness again.
If not to ease another's pain
then at least not to inflict more.
We are more than capable of goodness.
We have it in us.
We are more than capable of love.
Coax it out of us if necessary.
Be gentle.
More gentle than we are.
Amen.

✳ **53** ✳
. . . .

Psalm 109:26, 29-31

Help me, O Lord my God! Save me according to your steadfast love. May my accusers be clothed with dishonor; may they be wrapped in their own shame as in a mantle. With my mouth I will give great thanks to the Lord; I will praise him in the midst of the throng. For he stands at the right hand of the needy, to save them from those who would condemn them to death.

✳ 53 ✳
. . . .

"...may they be wrapped in their own shame."

Mirror, Mirror, God of all,
who's the fairest one of all?
We know when wrong has been done to us.
We want the guilty gagged and cuffed.
We want each one to feel our pain
and we want you to shame their name.
But just before they are erased,
show us the mirror of our face.
Remind us of when we were in their place,
we saw the reflection of your grace.
Mirror, Mirror, God of all,
you are the wisest one of all.
Amen

✳ 54 ✳

Ezekiel 30:18-20

I said to their children in the wilderness, Do
not follow the statutes of your parents, nor
observe their ordinances, nor defile yourselves
with their idols. I the Lord am your God;
follow my statutes, and be careful to observe
my ordinances, and hallow my sabbaths that
they may be a sign between me and you, so that
you may know that I the Lord am your God.

※ 54 ※

"...so that you may know that I the Lord am your God."

God of the So That,
we read these ancient texts
and are easily confused.
One text says 'Honor your parents'
and another says, 'Follow your parents' rules
unless your parents' rules are wrong.'
So, which is it?
We mean no disrespect, God.
We want to understand.
Sometimes we look for the 'so
that' in the sentences.
You always put something
important after the 'so that.'
Something about who we are and who you are
and who we are to you.
That helps.
Thank you for the so thats.
Amen.

※ 55 ※

John 1:47-51

When Jesus saw Nathanael coming towards him, he said of him, 'Here is truly an Israelite in whom there is no deceit!' Nathanael asked him, 'Where did you come to know me?' Jesus answered, 'I saw you under the fig tree before Philip called you.' Nathanael replied, 'Rabbi, you are the Son of God! You are the King of Israel!' [50]Jesus answered, 'Do you believe because I told you that I saw you under the fig tree? You will see greater things than these.' And he said to him, 'Very truly, I tell you, you will see heaven opened and the angels of God ascending and descending upon the Son of Man.'

✳ 55 ✳

"You will see greater things than these."

God of Way Up There,
we need you way down here.
God of Heaven, earth is waiting.
We are dutifully obeying the laws of gravity.
Our feet and our imagination are earth-bound.
You came here.
At least once. Maybe more. Who knows?
You brought your best
so that we could see even better.
So that we could see heaven and earth
not as two separate places but as one
moment, right now and again.
Help us to see greater things.
You can start with tapping us on the shoulder
and reminding us that you came a long time ago
and that you are still here.
Amen.

✳ **56** ✳
. . . .

Psalm 112:1-3

Praise the Lord! Happy are those who fear the
Lord, who greatly delight in his commandments.
Their descendants will be mighty in the
land; the generation of the upright will be
blessed. Wealth and riches are in their houses,
and their righteousness endures for ever.

※ 56 ※

"...riches are in their houses."

God of Pockets,
the richest people we know are
people with pockets
ready to be turned inside out,
ready to spill into hungry hands,
ready to feel a handful of blessings
poured out for the blessed poor.
Some of the richest people we know
don't have a dime to their name,
but they know they have a purpose
for their pockets just the same.
Designed to keep hands warm
ready to hold hands,
ready to love with the wealth of a touch.
The richest people we know,
know how to love with their pockets.
Amen

✳ 57 ✳
....

I Peter 4:7-11

The end of all things is near; therefore be serious and discipline yourselves for the sake of your prayers. Above all, maintain constant love for one another, for love covers a multitude of sins. Be hospitable to one another without complaining. Like good stewards of the manifold grace of God, serve one another with whatever gift each of you has received. Whoever speaks must do so as one speaking the very words of God; whoever serves must do so with the strength that God supplies, so that God may be glorified in all things through Jesus Christ. To him belong the glory and the power for ever and ever. Amen

✳ 57 ✳

**"like good stewards of the
manifold grace of God..."**

God of Physics and Fluid,
you pour yourself into us. The juices of your
grace fill us. We clench with fear of losing
what we have received. We leak. We evaporate.
We want to hoard the goodness for ourselves.
The fluidity of your love is designed
to flow through us.
If we contain what is not meant to be contained,
we become a physics lesson. A vacuum crushing
our own flesh to fill the empty space.
Your grace, O Lord, keeps pouring.
May we become a pouring chalice.
Fearless. Generous.
May we trust your flow to overflowing.
Let us become relentless springs
of uncontained grace.
Amen

※ 58 ※

Proverbs 21:24-26

The proud, haughty person, named 'Scoffer', acts with arrogant pride. The craving of the lazy person is fatal, for lazy hands refuse to labor. All day long the wicked covet, but the righteous give and do not hold back.

✳ 58 ✳

**"All day long the wicked covet,
but the righteous give..."**

Dear God,
what did you do today?
No, on second thought,
belay that request.
If we have to ask,
we haven't been paying attention.
It's not as if you work in secret all the time.
Chances are we were too occupied
with what we do not own.
What a way to waste a day
when we could have been
looking over your shoulder
and saying, "Wow!"
Wow is a much better way to spend a day.
Amen

✳ 59 ✳

He said also to the one who had invited him,
'When you give a luncheon or a dinner, do not
invite your friends or your brothers or your
relatives or rich neighbors, in case they may invite
you in return, and you would be repaid. But when
you give a banquet, invite the poor, the crippled,
the lame, and the blind. And you will be blessed,
because they cannot repay you, for you will be
repaid at the resurrection of the righteous.'

✳ 59 ✳
. . . .

**"Do not invite your friends...in case
they may invite you in return."**

God of our Great Expectations,
you understand the way we think
and lob little bricks wrapped in a message
that usually says, "Stop That."
We expect the golden rule to be golden to us.
We expect to be treated well
when we are generous and kind.
When we are not repaid
even with a thank you
our compassion collapses
under the weight of our disappointment.
Let our generosity be driven
by the needs of others.
Help us not to be strangled
in the strings attached to our expectations.
Amen

✳ **60** ✳
······················

Psalm 119:65-68

You have dealt well with your servant, O
Lord, according to your word. Teach me good
judgement and knowledge, for I believe in
your commandments. Before I was humbled I
went astray, but now I keep your word. You are
good and do good; teach me your statutes.

✳ **60** ✳
....

"...for I believe in your commandments."

Maker of Good Choices,
your commandments are a coat of many colors.
A fabric made of respect and love.
We are free to wear it,
to let the garment
change our pace and our posture,
to feel the heft and history of those
who have worn it before us,
to finger its frayed edge and torn places
carefully repaired.
Inside those clothes of commandments
we are free to choose how we shall live.
Let us choose wisely.
Let us wear your word well.
Amen

✳ 61 ✳
. . . .

I left you behind in Crete for this reason, that
you should put in order what remained to be
done, and should appoint elders in every town,
as I directed you: someone who is blameless,
married only once, whose children are believers,
not accused of debauchery and not rebellious. For
a bishop, as God's steward, must be blameless;
he must not be arrogant or quick-tempered or
addicted to wine or violent or greedy for gain;
but he must be hospitable, a lover of goodness,
prudent, upright, devout, and self-controlled.
He must have a firm grasp of the word that is
trustworthy in accordance with the teaching, so
that he may be able both to preach with sound
doctrine and to refute those who contradict it.

※ 61 ※

"...and he must be hospitable..."

Caller of Leaders,
it is our way to raise up leaders
in our midst by voice or vote.
You have always seen our need
for guardians of our hearts
and protectors of our days.
We can lift up those we wish.
Soak our wisdom in the water
of your words of grace,
your welcoming embrace.
May our leaders know their place
not as conquerors but servants
living in our midst.
Amen

✳ **62** ✳

Isaiah 57:14-16

It shall be said, 'Build up, build up, prepare the way, remove every obstruction from my people's way.' For thus says the high and lofty one who inhabits eternity, whose name is Holy: I dwell in the high and holy place, and also with those who are contrite and humble in spirit, to revive the spirit of the humble, and to revive the heart of the contrite. For I will not continually accuse, nor will I always be angry; for then the spirits would grow faint before me, even the souls that I have made.

⁜ **62** ⁜

**"...and also with those who are
contrite and humble..."**

God of the Stuck and the Stalled,
you bid your people to blaze trails,
to clear the path, to ford the flash floods,
and all the obstacles that stop us in our tracks.
Sometimes, we can't take another step.
We buckle.
We give in and give up
on ourselves and each other.
You choose to sit with us in our despair
and breathe the bitterness of our air
until we start to inhale the oxygen
of your belief in us.
We move to stand on wobbly hope
to continue on your way.
We humbly accept your hand.
Amen

⁜ 63 ⁜

Psalm 1: 1-3

Happy are those who do not follow the advice of the wicked, or take the path that sinners tread, or sit in the seat of scoffers; but their delight is in the law of the Lord, and on his law they meditate day and night. They are like trees planted by streams of water, which yield their fruit in its season, and their leaves do not wither. In all that they do, they prosper.

✳ **63** ✳
· · · · · · · · · · · · ·

"...like trees planted by streams of water..."

God of our porousness,
you are the best marinade.
You are as accessible as water to us
at least to many of us.
May your grace soak into us
and flavor our words and character.
We are either a poor influence to others
or easily influenced by those
who don't give a flip about us.
You care that we thrive and grow.
You plant us where we can stick our toes
in the river of your good name
to claim our birthright to the same.
Amen

※ **64** ※

Colossians 4: 7-9

Tychicus will tell you all the news about me;
he is a beloved brother, a faithful minister, and
a fellow-servant in the Lord. I have sent him
to you for this very purpose, so that you may
know how we are and that he may encourage
your hearts; he is coming with Onesimus, the
faithful and beloved brother, who is one of you.
They will tell you about everything here.

✖ **64** ✖
. . . .

"...and that he may encourage your hearts..."

Heart of Hearts,
when we get frightened, we stand still...
we freeze.
Our fingers and toes ration their blood supply
to keep our tiny hearts beating.
You invented the heart for courage.
Yes, more than just survival.
Yes, more than love.
Because life without courage is constant fear.
Because love without courage is empty.
At the end of the day and even at the beginning,
our hands and toes warm themselves
by your heart fire.
We reach with courageous hands
to help others live
and move on fearless feet to love.
Amen

✳ **65** ✳

Deuteronomy 29:10-13

You stand assembled today, all of you, before the
Lord your God—the leaders of your tribes, your
elders, and your officials, all the men of Israel,
your children, your women, and the aliens who
are in your camp, both those who cut your wood
and those who draw your water— to enter into
the covenant of the Lord your God, sworn by
an oath, which the Lord your God is making
with you today; in order that he may establish
you today as his people, and that he may be your
God, as he promised you and as he swore to your
ancestors, to Abraham, to Isaac, and to Jacob.

❋ 65 ❋
. . . .

"...to enter into the covenant...which the Lord your God is making with you today."

God of Today,
you are seen
among the stories of ancient ones.
You are seen
among the stories of those who messed up.
You renew your promises.
You cast out threads
we can use to tie ourselves together
or tie around our fingers
to remember what you said.
What you promised.
Make this day
another today in which you enter
even while we are still rubbing our eyes
wondering how we got here.
Amen

✳ **66** ✳

Luke 14:31-33

Or what king, going out to wage war against
another king, will not sit down first and
consider whether he is able with ten thousand
to oppose the one who comes against him
with twenty thousand? If he cannot, then,
while the other is still far away, he sends a
delegation and asks for the terms of peace. So
therefore, none of you can become my disciple
if you do not give up all your possessions.

✖ **66** ✖
. . . .

**"...he sends a delegation and asks
for the terms of peace..."**

God of our Stuff,
you have wrestled with the grip
we have on our possessions.
We cling to things
that preserve our way of life.
Sooner or later we are threatened
By power. By change.
By so much outside of our control.
Our grip tightens.
We choose our fights poorly.
What would we be willing to give up
not to die today?
What would we be willing to give up
to keep our neighbor alive another day?
We are so tired of wrestling.
May we use what energy we have
for the greater good and good night's sleep.
Amen

✳ **67** ✳

Psalm 101:1-3

I will sing of loyalty and of justice; to you, O Lord,
I will sing. I will study the way that is blameless.
When shall I attain it? I will walk with integrity
of heart within my house; I will not set before
my eyes anything that is base. I hate the work of
those who fall away; it shall not cling to me.

✳ **67** ✳
. . . .

**"I will walk with integrity of
heart within my house."**

God of inside and out,
holy are you and wholesome.
No hidden agenda.
You establish a way of living
steeped in justice and tenderness.
You call us to holy lives,
to move seamlessly from public to private
and back again.
That is integrity.
Help us to be at peace inside our own skin.
Even among our own kin.
Even in our own house.
Even when we are alone.
Teach us to wear our hearts on our sleeves
and trust all that is inside and out
to your tender care.
Amen

✳ **68** ✳
. . . .

I Timothy 4:6-8

If you put these instructions before the brothers
and sisters, you will be a good servant of Christ
Jesus, nourished on the words of the faith and
of the sound teaching that you have followed.
Have nothing to do with profane myths and
old wives' tales. Train yourself in godliness, for,
while physical training is of some value, godliness
is valuable in every way, holding promise for
both the present life and the life to come.

✳ **68** ✳

"...godliness is valuable in every way."

Good Mentor,
though not without merit,
your choice of topic could have been
(forgive us) less boring.
That is what we do with godliness.
We yawn.
We reduce it to cleanliness,
to a household chore,
to avoiding the curse-word-du-jour.
We imagine goodness as dull and a
pinch of evil as the spice of life.
This is the debris field that
godliness has to navigate.
May we muck out our less than mature minds
to have room for your good stuff.
Amen

✖ **69** ✖
. . . .

A certain ruler asked him, 'Good Teacher, what must I do to inherit eternal life?' Jesus said to him, 'Why do you call me good? No one is good but God alone. You know the commandments: "You shall not commit adultery; You shall not murder; You shall not steal; You shall not bear false witness; Honor your father and mother." ' He replied, 'I have kept all these since my youth.' When Jesus heard this, he said to him, 'There is still one thing lacking. Sell all that you own and distribute the money to the poor, and you will have treasure in heaven; then come, follow me.'

※ 69 ※

"I have kept all these [commandments] since my youth."

Dear Jesus,
How did you keep from laughing?
Seriously.
Did Luke decide to leave out your explosive
guffaw or your muffled snicker?
The question posed to you that day
has been eternally repeated.
What must we DO for eternal life?
Your answer was...basically...walk with me.
Don't pack anything that will weigh us down.
Help anyone else from falling behind.
We are silly to think this journey is a race
with a prize at the end.
The journey is the destination.
You have a right to laugh.
Thanks for letting us tag along.
We are, at least, good for laugh.
Amen

✻ 70 ✻
. . . .

Psalm 51:1-4

Have mercy on me, O God, according to your
steadfast love; according to your abundant mercy
blot out my transgressions. Wash me thoroughly
from my iniquity, and cleanse me from my sin.
For I know my transgressions, and my sin is
ever before me. Against you, you alone, have
I sinned, and done what is evil in your sight,
so that you are justified in your sentence
and blameless when you pass judgement.

※ 70 ※

**"...blot out my transgressions,
wash me thoroughly..."**

Lord of our Laundromat,
from our sisters in time
who stood with river rocks
to washboards,
to tubs with wringers,
to clothes lines,
to pick a cycle, size, and heat, to tumble dry.
To all who labor to blot out
our little transgressions
and the stink of our days and ways.
To all who know it never ends
the soiling, the washing, the drying, the
folding, the putting away only to start again.
God, you understand the aching shoulders
of washer women
as you stand hip deep in our murky humanity.
Wring us clean and dry.
Have we ever thanked you?
Amen

✳ 71 ✳

Noah was six hundred years old when the flood of waters came on the earth. And Noah with his sons and his wife and his sons' wives went into the ark to escape the waters of the flood. Of clean animals, and of animals that are not clean, and of birds, and of everything that creeps on the ground, two and two, male and female, went into the ark with Noah, as God had commanded Noah. And after seven days the waters of the flood came on the earth.

※ 71 ※

"...the waters of the flood..."

God of Too Much, Too Soon, Too Fast,
we are the overwhelmed.
The ones caught in the undertow.
We are the ones ignoring
the warnings in the dry riverbed
until the thunder flashes
overhead and underfoot.
We are the bags of flesh made of water,
needing water and swept away by just too much.
We are the ones still alive to see the aftermath.
We are the ones mucking out, drying out,
looking for a reason not to drown in the despair.
God of Noah,
keep sending boats.
Amen.

✳ 72 ✳
. . . .

Genesis 8: 20-22

Then Noah built an altar to the Lord, and took
of every clean animal and of every clean bird,
and offered burnt-offerings on the altar. And
when the Lord smelt the pleasing odor, the
Lord said in his heart, 'I will never again curse
the ground because of humankind, for the
inclination of the human heart is evil from youth;
nor will I ever again destroy every living creature
as I have done. As long as the earth endures,
seedtime and harvest, cold and heat, summer
and winter, day and night, shall not cease.'

✳ 72 ✳
. . . .

**"As long as the earth endures, seedtime
and harvest...shall not cease."**

Eternal God of Constant Change,
you created a fluid world
of seasons, time, light and temperature.
You created us floating and finding land
and setting off to sea again.
Uncertainty is a way of life.
And still we strap ourselves to the mast
hoping for stillness in the storms of change.
What endures is the motion.
We find a still point
when we are aware of who we are
and who we are not.
We find a still point
when the sun rises
and finds us utterly surprised by another day.
Amen

✳ 73 ✳
. . . .

So he told them this parable: 'Which one of you, having a hundred sheep and losing one of them, does not leave the ninety-nine in the wilderness and go after the one that is lost until he finds it? When he has found it, he lays it on his shoulders and rejoices. And when he comes home, he calls together his friends and neighbors, saying to them, "Rejoice with me, for I have found my sheep that was lost." Just so, I tell you, there will be more joy in heaven over one sinner who repents than over ninety-nine righteous people who need no repentance.

※ 73 ※

"...he lays it on his shoulders and rejoices."

Shepherd of the Ninety-Nine,
we probably didn't notice you were gone until
we saw you coming back. One riding on your
shoulders, wrapped around your neck.
If your humans were really like
sheep, we wouldn't care.
We care about eating and not being eaten
and that's about it.
We hear this story told to your human flock.
We confess a twinge of envy.
How the prodigal sheep is lifted up
and gets a ride and a party.
And centuries later would come all the
sculptures, the paintings, the stained
glass windows of you with that one
on your shoulders.
The rest of us just looking for lunch.
May our turn come to find ourselves
on shoulders big enough for us all.
Amen

✳ **74** ✳
. . . .

Psalm 73:26-28

My flesh and my heart may fail, but God is the
strength of my heart and my portion forever.
Indeed, those who are far from you will perish;
you put an end to those who are false to you. But
for me it is good to be near God; I have made the
Lord God my refuge, to tell of all your works.

✳ 74 ✳
· · · · · · · · · · · · · ·

"But for me it is good to be near God."

Oh, Hi!
How long have you been here?
When did you arrive? How was your trip?
Have a seat.
It is so good. It is so good.
It is so good to be with you.
You are like those friends who we haven't
seen for a long time but when we do
the time between us evaporates into a holy now.
Has it ever been bad to be with you?
Sometimes your communication
staff doesn't speak well for you.
We are all guilty of that.
But you are here and near.
We are so grateful.
Thank you for coming
and mending the gap that
we let grow between us.
Amen

✳ 75 ✳
· · · · · · · · · · · · · ·

Jonah 3:6-10

When the news reached the king of Nineveh, he rose from his throne, removed his robe, covered himself with sackcloth, and sat in ashes. Then he had a proclamation made in Nineveh: 'By the decree of the king and his nobles: No human being or animal, no herd or flock, shall taste anything. They shall not feed, nor shall they drink water. Human beings and animals shall be covered with sackcloth, and they shall cry mightily to God. All shall turn from their evil ways and from the violence that is in their hands. Who knows? God may relent and change his mind; he may turn from his fierce anger, so that we do not perish.' When God saw what they did, how they turned from their evil ways, God changed his mind about the calamity that he had said he would bring upon them; and he did not do it.

✳ 75 ✳
. . . .

"...God changed his mind..."

God of Cause and Effect,
your whole collection of stories
that we wrote down
and numbered each verse
and bound in leather
feels like riding a pendulum
between action and reaction.
The world was made. We messed it up.
You made clothes for the messy ones.
We hoped for the best.
You warned your people with consequences.
You changed your mind.
We rode our relationship
while it swung
between our thoughtlessness
and your mindfulness.
We would be glad for a little less motion.
Steady as she goes, your grace.
Amen.

✳ 76 ✳

John 3:13-17

No one has ascended into heaven except the
one who descended from heaven, the Son of
Man. And just as Moses lifted up the serpent
in the wilderness, so must the Son of Man be
lifted up, that whoever believes in him may have
eternal life. 'For God so loved the world that he
gave his only Son, so that everyone who believes
in him may not perish but may have eternal
life. 'Indeed, God did not send the Son into
the world to condemn the world, but in order
that the world might be saved through him.

※ 76 ※

"...so must the Son of Man be lifted up..."

God of Giggling Babies,
It was you, wasn't it?
It was you who invented that game
so many parents play with infants
after the babes can raise their own
heads and recognize the face.
The game is a simple one.
To toss the child in the air a few inches
or more beyond the tosser's fingers
and catch them firmly.
All the while the child's wide-open mouth
speaks delight in a child's first language
of gurgle, squeak and spit.
Over the years, we may have forgotten the
game of lifting up as you intended.
We gave it a much darker tone.
We can find your game again
within your reach, your fingers, your face.
We can learn to laugh again.
Amen

❈ 77 ❈

Psalm 113:5-8

Who is like the Lord our God, who is seated on
high, who looks far down on the heavens and
the earth? He raises the poor from the dust, and
lifts the needy from the ash heap, to make them
sit with princes, with the princes of his people.

※ 77 ※

"...and lifts the needy from the ash heap..."

Weightlifter,
there you go...lifting little ones up again.
This time you are lifting the ones
who need the weight of the world
off their shoulders.
We see the needy ones too.
But we feel our fatigue and our own weakness.
Their weight is beyond our weight limit.
But not our class.
We can walk away or start small.
We can lift a little one
a cup of water,
a hand to hold,
a voice that says their name out loud
so they know they are seen as
diamonds in a rough world.
As one of us.
As loved.
Amen

✳ 78 ✳

Romans 8:31-34

What then are we to say about these things? If God is for us, who is against us? He who did not withhold his own Son, but gave him up for all of us, will he not with him also give us everything else? Who will bring any charge against God's elect? It is God who justifies. Who is to condemn? It is Christ Jesus, who died, yes, who was raised, who is at the right hand of God, who indeed intercedes for us.

❊ 78 ❊
· · · · · · · · · · · · ·

"If God is for us, who is against us?"

Good Sport,
you hear your name in locker rooms
asking to bless the competition
and bless us a little more than them.
We want to win...to bring you glory...of course.
We have embraced the lie
of us or them.
of win or lose.
of you must have your favorites.
As we play this game, lives are lost.
There is no victor.
There is you and there is us.
That's all.
That's everything.
Amen

✳ 79 ✳
. . . .

He sat down opposite the treasury, and watched the crowd putting money into the treasury. Many rich people put in large sums. A poor widow came and put in two small copper coins, which are worth a penny. Then he called his disciples and said to them, 'Truly I tell you, this poor widow has put in more than all those who are contributing to the treasury. For all of them have contributed out of their abundance; but she out of her poverty has put in everything she had, all she had to live on.'

※ 79 ※

"...Jesus sat down...and watched the crowd."

Crowd-watcher,
you saw the rich people with large offerings.
They were easy to see.
You saw one woman with a couple of pennies.
You called your friends to you
and told them what you saw.
You, O Lord, are the lens for us
to see what we are missing.
To see who we are missing.
Bless our people-watching
with fewer filters,
with more compassion,
with fresh insight.
Amen

✳ 80 ✳
. . . .

'Whoever is faithful in a very little is faithful also in much; and whoever is dishonest in a very little is dishonest also in much. If then you have not been faithful with the dishonest wealth, who will entrust to you the true riches? And if you have not been faithful with what belongs to another, who will give you what is your own? No slave can serve two masters; for a slave will either hate the one and love the other, or be devoted to the one and despise the other. You cannot serve God and wealth.'

※ 80 ※

"You cannot serve God and wealth."

Holy God of homeowner associations,
you've had a lot to say over the years
about what we own
and what owns us
and how we treat our neighbors.
We get defensive.
We are quick to declare ourselves good neighbors
until we get too busy, too tired,
too concerned about the resale value
or where our pets' poo.
Our goodness trips on little things.
Help us to love our neighbors.
Really love them.
Amen

✻ **81** ✻

Psalm 12:5-7

'Because the poor are despoiled, because the
needy groan, I will now rise up,' says the Lord; 'I
will place them in the safety for which they long.'
The promises of the Lord are promises that are
pure, silver refined in a furnace on the ground,
purified seven times. You, O Lord, will protect us;
you will guard us from this generation forever.

✳ 81 ✳
. . . .

**"The promises of the Lord are...
purified seven times."**

Singer,
the song of your teaching has a familiar refrain -
to regard the poor. To see their need.
To respond with compassion.
The song plays over and over again.
We are slow learners.
The message refrains, reframes, repeats.
Until it breaks through
even one ear at a time.
One mind. One heart.
Until we hear it with thunder in our chests.
Until we say, "Oh, maybe we should do
something grows into we can do something.
The poor with us always
is not an excuse to do nothing
but a reason to repeat the refrain of love...
for the rest of our lives.
Amen

✳ 82 ✳

I Corinthians 9:19-23

For though I am free with respect to all, I have
made myself a slave to all, so that I might win
more of them. To the Jews I became as a Jew,
in order to win Jews. To those under the law I
became as one under the law (though I myself
am not under the law) so that I might win those
under the law. To those outside the law I became
as one outside the law (though I am not free from
God's law but am under Christ's law) so that I
might win those outside the law. To the weak I
became weak, so that I might win the weak. I have
become all things to all people, so that I might
by any means save some. I do it all for the sake of
the gospel, so that I may share in its blessings.

✳ 82 ✳

**"I do it all for the gospel so that
I may share in its blessing."**

Dear Paul,
You were the rock star of your day.
You were full of yourself
and so sure you were right until you
had your come-to-Jesus moment.
A few years impaired and cared for
by those you loathed left you changed.
We imagine you spent that time listening
more than posting your opinions.
You would still be at odds at times
with Peter and women
and Rome
which tied you up in your time and in ours.
Yet, your mail still gets picked up and read.
And even though you are dead
you share in the blessing of grace.
We believe that in part because you did.
Rock on, Brother Paul, rock on.
Amen

✳ 83 ✳
. . . .

Matthew 9:9-13

As Jesus was walking along, he saw a man called
Matthew sitting at the tax booth; and he said to
him, 'Follow me.' And he got up and followed
him. And as he sat at dinner in the house,
many tax-collectors and sinners came and were
sitting with him and his disciples. When the
Pharisees saw this, they said to his disciples,
'Why does your teacher eat with tax-collectors
and sinners?' But when he heard this, he said,
'Those who are well have no need of a physician,
but those who are sick. Go and learn what this
means, "I desire mercy, not sacrifice." For I have
come to call not the righteous but sinners.'

※ 83 ※

"I desire mercy, not sacrifice."

Dinner Companion,
you never ate alone.
You went alone to pray sometimes,
but eating was a peopled event.
Often a motley bunch of opportunists
and fan boys mixed in
with faces that say, "I'm fine. No, really,
I'm fine. Would you like more to eat?"
You saw everyone at the table
and the wait staff and more.
You see the needs, the bleeding out,
the sweeping up.
Mercy is a different way of dining.
Amen

※ 84 ※

Psalm 146:5-7a

Happy are those whose help is the God of Jacob, whose hope is in the Lord their God, who made heaven and earth, the sea, and all that is in them; who keeps faith forever; who executes justice for the oppressed; who gives food to the hungry. The Lord sets the prisoners free.

※ 84 ※
. . . .

"...who gives food to the hungry."

Supply Chain Manager,
we are a needy nest of cheeping souls.
Some too young or old to manage without help.
Some too tired to do much.
Some too cruel to share.
You offer endless shipments
of help, hope, heaven and earth.
You pay attention to food deserts
and service denied.
We are the needy and the fed.
We are the source of your plenty
and the supply chain.
IF we choose to be.
If we choose to be...a link in the chain.
Amen

✳ 85 ✳

Proverbs 28: 6-8

Better to be poor and walk in integrity than
to be crooked in one's ways even though rich.
Those who keep the law are wise children, but
companions of gluttons shame their parents.
One who augments wealth by exorbitant interest
gathers it for another who is kind to the poor.

※ 85 ※

**"Better to be poor and walk in integrity...
than to be crooked in one's ways..."**

Wise One,
there are so many other possibilities.
Poor and crooked.
Rich and righteous.
Getting by and tell the captain to move
the yacht into international waters.
There is really poor and there is really crooked.
We could argue that our wealth,
especially our lack of it, is not a choice at all.
Our crookedness?
Okay, we give you that. That is a choice.
No matter our lot in life,
lead us not into the temptation of
putting our integrity up for sale.
Amen.

※ 86 ※

Proverbs 28:25-28

The greedy person stirs up strife, but whoever trusts in the Lord will be enriched. Those who trust in their own wits are fools; but those who walk in wisdom come through safely. Whoever gives to the poor will lack nothing, but one who turns a blind eye will get many a curse. When the wicked prevail, people go into hiding; but when they perish, the righteous increase.

※ 86 ※

**"...whoever trusts in the Lord
will be enriched."**

Oh God,
you call us to wisdom, to generosity,
but this call to trust you is a problem.
We have trust issues.
We have so many lesser things that
give us temporary comfort.
We tend to think that trusting you
is our last resort
when all else fails including our comfort things.
One of these days we will take our last breath
and then what? Is that when our trust kicks
in? We would really like to trust you now,
but sometimes we don't know how.
Oh, God, we want to trust you in this life
during the living of these days.
Coax us out of hiding.
Help us believe.
Amen

✳ 87 ✳

'There was a rich man who was dressed in purple and fine linen and who feasted sumptuously every day. And at his gate lay a poor man named Lazarus, covered with sores, who longed to satisfy his hunger with what fell from the rich man's table; even the dogs would come and lick his sores. The poor man died and was carried away by the angels to be with Abraham. The rich man also died and was buried. In Hades, where he was being tormented, he looked up and saw Abraham far away with Lazarus by his side.

✳ 87 ✳
. . . .

**"...who longed to satisfy his hunger with
what fell from the rich man's table..."**

God of Maslow's Pyramid,
the hierarchy of human needs: transcendence,
self-actualization, aesthetics, cognition,
esteem, belonging, safety, physiological.
These are high scoring scrabble words
between holy and hungry.
The danger of a mountain of human need
is that it can become
a cruel game of King of the Mountain.
And many of us are caught
in between the need and the power play.
Level the field, O God,
and let us first learn to be
beggars sharing our bread.
Amen

※ 88 ※

Psalm 62: 5-7

For God alone my soul waits in silence, for
my hope is from him. He alone is my rock
and my salvation, my fortress; I shall not be
shaken. On God rests my deliverance and my
honor; my mighty rock, my refuge is in God.

※ 88 ※

"...my mighty rock, my refuge..."

Geode,
that's a good nickname for you.
We need metaphors
to wrap our heads around who you are.
You are like rocks - not to throw -
But more like foundations
for pathways and waterways, for safe ways.
A mighty metaphor to shelter our fear.
When our lives shift like the earth under our
feet like the ocean surf reclaiming the sand we
stand upon, we long for solid ground, for rock.
You are rock.
If you really were a geode, we would be
tempted to crack you open to know your
hidden secrets and claim your treasure.
Give us the strength to stand still
especially when we are afraid.
May we be held inside the strength of
your mystery as your treasure.
Amen

✳ 89 ✳

James 5:1-6

Come now, you rich people, weep and wail for the miseries that are coming to you. Your riches have rotted, and your clothes are moth-eaten. Your gold and silver have rusted, and their rust will be evidence against you, and it will eat your flesh like fire. You have laid up treasure for the last days. Listen! The wages of the laborers who mowed your fields, which you kept back by fraud, cry out, and the cries of the harvesters have reached the ears of the Lord of hosts. You have lived on the earth in luxury and in pleasure; you have fattened your hearts on a day of slaughter. You have condemned and murdered the righteous one, who does not resist you.

※ 89 ※

"Come now, you rich people..."

James, Son of Shame,
we pick through your letter like a buffet table.
Some words are tasty.
Some passages make good fighting words
for those who we see as all talk and no walk.
We pass on the kale
that tells us the bitter truth about ourselves
no matter how it is prepared.
Shame is the new curse word.
We don't want anyone looking at our
plates while we are looking at theirs.
We are picky eaters.
You were brave, James,
to serve us the truth anyway.
May we have a bon appetite.
Amen

✳ 90 ✳

Hosea 12:2-6

The Lord has an indictment against Judah, and will punish Jacob according to his ways, and repay him according to his deeds. In the womb he tried to supplant his brother, and in his manhood he strove with God. He strove with the angel and prevailed, he wept and sought his favor; he met him at Bethel, and there he spoke with him. The Lord the God of hosts, the Lord is his name! But as for you, return to your God, hold fast to love and justice, and wait continually for your God.

✳ 90 ✳
. . . .

"But as for you, return to your God...and wait."
Wait, what? God?
We are to return to you and then wait for you?
Respectfully, God,
this is the kind of thing that makes
faith feel like running in circles chasing our tail.
Is it virtue signaling to say we are
seeking you, chasing you?
Is it closer to the truth that you are
chasing us...sometimes over a cliff?
Do you mind if we slow down a bit
and maybe sit?
What we need will come to us.
Amen

✳ 91 ✳

And war broke out in heaven; Michael and his
angels fought against the dragon. The dragon
and his angels fought back, but they were
defeated, and there was no longer any place for
them in heaven. The great dragon was thrown
down, that ancient serpent, who is called the
Devil and Satan, the deceiver of the whole
world—he was thrown down to the earth, and
his angels were thrown down with him.

※ 91 ※

**"...and Satan...he was thrown down to
the earth and his angels...with him."**

Revealer, you inspired a guy alone
on a Greek island to write a book
that the rest of us clamor to decode
or worse...take at face value as spooky non-fiction.
We ask questions like "Where did evil come from?"
because it couldn't be our fault.
We are enchanted by heroes and
dragons in a distant war
until we learn we are in the thick of it.
So making it all your fault makes sense. Right?
Or maybe we are missing something.
Reveal to us what we need to see.
There is evil and there is heaven and earth.
We're in this together, God.
We're in this together.
Amen

✳ 92 ✳

2 Kings 19:15-19

And Hezekiah prayed before the Lord, and said:
'O Lord the God of Israel, who are enthroned
above the cherubim, you are God, you alone, of all
the kingdoms of the earth; you have made heaven
and earth. Incline your ear, O Lord, and hear;
open your eyes, O Lord, and see; hear the words
of Sennacherib, which he has sent to mock the
living God. Truly, O Lord, the kings of Assyria
have laid waste the nations and their lands, and
have hurled their gods into the fire, though they
were no gods but the work of human hands—
wood and stone—and so they were destroyed. So
now, O Lord our God, save us, I pray you, from
his hand, so that all the kingdoms of the earth
may know that you, O Lord, are God alone.'

※ 92 ※

**"So now, O Lord God, save us...
from his hand..."**

Karaoke God,
we sing familiar songs at the tipsy-top of our fear.
We hold the mic and belt out
"We need a HERO-OOOOOO. We're holdin'
out for a hero 'til the end of the night."
We always want heroes.
We asked for kings. You weren't
crazy about the idea.
You gave us kings anyway. We waxed cold
on monarchs, but we still look for saviors.
We lump Jesus into our fire-insurance policy.
He wasn't the kind of hero we were hoping for.
What if Jesus came not to be
the one and only hero?
What if Jesus came to show us how
to be larger than our lives?
Amen

✳ 93 ✳

Matthew 20:29-34

As they were leaving Jericho, a large crowd followed him. There were two blind men sitting by the roadside. When they heard that Jesus was passing by, they shouted, 'Lord, have mercy on us, Son of David!' The crowd sternly ordered them to be quiet; but they shouted even more loudly, 'Have mercy on us, Lord, Son of David!' Jesus stood still and called them, saying, 'What do you want me to do for you?' They said to him, 'Lord, let our eyes be opened.' Moved with compassion, Jesus touched their eyes. Immediately they regained their sight and followed him.

※ 93 ※

"Have mercy on us, Lord..."

Have mercy, Lord.
Sitting on the side of the road
without being able to see
with others who can't see
is not where we want to be.
The crowd stirs up road dust and dismisses us.
You stood still.
You saw us when we could not see you.
You spoke. You asked us what we wanted.
Is sight too much to ask?
Apparently not. We see you.
We're on our feet.
We're following.
Help us to have mercy
on those we see along the way.
Amen

✳ 94 ✳

Luke 17:5-6

The apostles said to the Lord, 'Increase our
faith!' The Lord replied, 'If you had faith
the size of a mustard seed, you could say
to this mulberry tree, "Be uprooted and
planted in the sea", and it would obey you.

✻ 94 ✻

"...if you had faith the size of a mustard seed..."

Christ,
we wring these verses
into cheap jewelry and refrigerator magnets.
We understand the need for bigger faith.
We compare ourselves to...well...you.
We don't measure up. So, we ask for
more. You tell us we have enough.
The deadest, smallest seed knows how to grow.
Faith is trusting that seed enough
to drop it on the earth.
Faith is whispering to it
even in our uncertainty:
'Now, go and grow. Be a tree or whatever.'
Oh, okay.
Amen

✳ 95 ✳

Psalm 3:5-8

I lie down and sleep; I wake again, for the Lord sustains me. I am not afraid of tens of thousands of people who have set themselves against me all around. Rise up, O Lord! Deliver me, O my God! For you strike all my enemies on the cheek; you break the teeth of the wicked. Deliverance belongs to the Lord; may your blessing be on your people!

✳ 95 ✳
············

"I lie down and sleep; I wake again..."

God of Slumber,
now, you're talkin'!
Sleep. Yes. Now, please.
We need the kind that starts
at the moment our cheeks feel sheets.
The kind that keeps our minds
from replaying the coulda, shoulda,
woulda scenes of the past.
The kind that lets our drama drift
where we know we will find it again tomorrow.
The sleep that lets our fear go numb
and lets our muscles rest.
The kind that believes there will be a new day
and you'll be there with us to see it.
Amen

※ 96 ※

I John 5:1-5

Everyone who believes that Jesus is the Christ has been born of God, and everyone who loves the parent loves the child. By this we know that we love the children of God, when we love God and obey his commandments. For the love of God is this, that we obey his commandments. And his commandments are not burdensome, for whatever is born of God conquers the world. And this is the victory that conquers the world, our faith. Who is it that conquers the world but the one who believes that Jesus is the Son of God?

✳ **96** ✳
. . . .

**"And this is the victory that
conquers the world, our faith."**

God of our childishness,
our earth is beautiful and glistens
with your creative imagination however...
the world does need to be conquered.
The human part feels caught in
perpetual toddler mode.
Pick a human century and there we are
in a tantrum, arching our backs
on the face of the earth
in blood-curdling disobedience.
You, Lord, have the wisdom and strength
of a first-grade teacher.
You don't give up on the difficult child
and you don't give in on the house rules.
You gave us those rules to help us
to rule our world with respect and love.
Help us to conquer the world
with everyday acts of faith.
Amen

✳ 97 ✳

....

Habakkuk 2:12-14

'Alas for you who build a town by bloodshed, and found a city on iniquity!' Is it not from the Lord of hosts that peoples labor only to feed the flames, and nations weary themselves for nothing? But the earth will be filled with the knowledge of the glory of the Lord, as the waters cover the sea.

❇ 97 ❇

**"...filled with the knowledge of
the glory of the Lord."**

Fountainhead,
we have been left parched and empty by our fill
of self-serving,
of whining and war,
of weary words,
of smoldering fear,
of provocateurs,
of flame feeders.
You, O God, are the filler of the oceans
and our emptiness.
Cool our tempers
Quench our thirst for truth to overflowing.
and hydrate our hope.
Amen

✳ 98 ✳

Psalm 111:1-3

Praise the Lord! I will give thanks to the Lord with my whole heart, in the company of the upright, in the congregation. Great are the works of the Lord, studied by all who delight in them. Full of honor and majesty is his work, and his righteousness endures forever.

✳ **98** ✳

"I will give thanks to the Lord
with my whole heart..."
God of Everything and the Kitchen Sink,
it takes less than a blink
to see something we didn't make.
A pelican. A blade of grass. A neighborhood
car. A mountain of cloud
and the likes of us.
Our senses fire with creation's wonders.
Our fog dampens our amazement
until we remember you.
Until we exude a bit of gratitude.
And when our gratitude grows
into a full-throated, whole-hearted howl of delight,
then, O Lord,
we begin to live.
Amen

✳ 99 ✳
. . . .

The Lord spoke to Moses, saying: Command
the Israelites to put out of the camp everyone
who is leprous, or has a discharge, and everyone
who is unclean through contact with a corpse;
you shall put out both male and female, putting
them outside the camp; they must not defile their
camp, where I dwell among them. The Israelites
did so, putting them outside the camp; as the
Lord had spoken to Moses, so the Israelites did.

✳ 99 ✳
. . . .

"...you shall put out both male and female..."

Public Service Announcer,
it took us a while to figure out
that public health is...well, public.
Before there were microscopes to see them,
germs jumped from one person to another.
And so we are dependent
from one person to another for our safety.
Forgive us for spending too much time arguing
what men can do and what women should do.
Help us to see that we are equally capable
of spreading disease and saving lives.
Amen

✳ 100 ✳

Once, when he was in one of the cities, there was a man covered with leprosy. When he saw Jesus, he bowed with his face to the ground and begged him, 'Lord, if you choose, you can make me clean.' Then Jesus stretched out his hand, touched him, and said, 'I do choose. Be made clean.' Immediately the leprosy left him. And he ordered him to tell no one. 'Go', he said, 'and show yourself to the priest, and, as Moses commanded, make an offering for your cleansing, for a testimony to them.' But now more than ever the word about Jesus spread abroad; many crowds would gather to hear him and to be cured of their diseases. But he would withdraw to deserted places and pray.

✳ 100 ✳
. . . .

**"...crowds would gather to hear him and
be cured. But he would withdraw..."**

AWOL Jesus,
all it took was a touch from you
and a hideous disease was cured.
The more you cured the more the
word spread like a disease.
You left.
You left to pray
and then you left for good.
So here we are sitting alone and lonely
trying to figure out how to live without you.
So here we are talking with you.
How is that withdrawing draws you close?
How is it that you figured out how
to touch us all at once?
You are smarter than we give you credit.
Amen

✳ 100+1 ✳

Luke 17:12-16

As he entered a village, ten lepers approached him.
Keeping their distance, they called out, saying,
'Jesus, Master, have mercy on us!' When he saw
them, he said to them, 'Go and show yourselves
to the priests.' And as they went, they were made
clean. Then one of them, when he saw that he
was healed, turned back, praising God with a
loud voice. He prostrated himself at Jesus' feet
and thanked him. And he was a Samaritan.

※ 100+1 ※

"And he was a Samaritan."

Holy Ground of the Least Likely,
the sick ones kept their distance.
It was the law. They were obedient.
You skipped to the good part and sent
them away to get their seal of approval.
One closed the distance between him and the
only priest that mattered. The only one to thank.
He was no longer a sick one,
but still the kind from whom people kept their
distance because he was not one of them.
He was the least-likely. The least-likely to believe
correctly. The least-likely to worship well. The least-
likely to obey the rules. The least-likely to stop and
help a stranger. At least, that's what was thought.
May we who see ourselves as the least-likely to
amount to anything and those who are seen by
others as unacceptable stand grateful, barefooted
on holy ground, and welcome in your presence
with all the other least-likely folks.
Amen

About the Author

Deb Grant is a human living under the laws of gravity in Houston, Texas. Grant is the author of 9 previous books, Pedestrian Theology, ELOGOS Daily Devotions for Down to Earth Disciples 1, 2, & 3, Passage: Lenten Devotions, Storm, Nuevo Vino, Wellspring Simple and contributing author to Beacon Hunters.

A native of New England, Grant earned her undergraduate degree from Barrington College (now Gordon College). She earned a Master of Divinity from Trinity Lutheran Seminary, Columbus, Ohio. Grant was ordained in 1981, serving as a pastor in the Evangelical Lutheran Church in America in Goodlettsville, Tennessee; Clemson, South Carolina; College Station, Texas and Dickinson, Texas. After 37 years in parish and campus ministry, Grant retired. She continues to write, create art pieces, care for her friends, and use her art and words whenever possible for the greater good. Most of the time she is the humble servant to her dog and bird.

Deb Grant's Contact Information:

Email: revdeb@jazzwater.com

Websites: jazzwater.com

debgrant.substack.com

Etsy Shop: www.etsy.com/shop/Jazzwater

Facebook: elogosbydebgrant

Instagram: jazzwater

To purchase Deb Grant's books:

Jazzwater.com

Independent bookstores

Amazon.com

CPSIA information can be obtained
at www.ICGtesting.com
Printed in the USA
JSHW010931151022
31627JS00005B/18

9 781737 218104